101 Behavior Tips for Parents

Richard Curtis

2nd edition

ISBN-13: 978-1499532111
ISBN-10: 1499532113

DEDICATION

"Holding onto anger is like grasping a hot coal with the intent of throwing it at someone else; you are the one who gets burned."

Buddha

Head on over to

101tipsforparents.com

for an exclusive thank you gift from

The Kid Calmer.

Richard Curtis

Recognizing anger, the lion inside you

A lion makes you:

- Want to prowl (you are hot and restless with hunched shoulders and neck);
- Want to look mean (your facial expression shows it, your fists are clenched);
- Want to feel powerful (you are unable to think clearly and you want control of your brain and the brains of the 'prey' around you);
- Prepared to fight (you have a knot in their stomach and are sick, your muscles are tense ready for the fight);
- Prepared to defend your pride (you feel that you are right and will defend your view);
- Prepared to strike (you are ready to pounce on the weakest prey that shows themselves).

Look out for anger management tips for lion taming throughout the book.

Richard Curtis

1. Don't see the behavior, see your child trying to solve a problem with the wrong tools.

2. Never give up on your child! If you give up, who else will care?

3. Consider a change of environment to help get out of a meltdown.

4. Build a child up for succeeding; make them feel on top of the world. That way they won't seek that feeling through negative behavior.

5. It only takes a small change in what you say to have a large change in your children's' behavior. Use "what would you like to do after tidying your room?" instead of "tidy your room".

6. Doing a jigsaw puzzle is a brilliant way of giving our brain space to think and calm down. There are loads of other similar activities, like dot-to-dot, sewing, tic-tac-toe, solitaire. What similar activities would work for your children?

7. Offer possible solutions your child could choose to scaffold their way out of a situation. You could offer to help your child to tidy their room if they want.

8. Having clear family rules means expectations in your house are clear.

9. The purpose of teaching a child positive behaviors is that they become natural as they grow up, just like manners.

10. Lion taming - offering your child possible solutions to what makes them angry helps tame the lion.

11. Some children like stickers on a chart, some like them on their chest, some like them on the back of their bedroom door. How publicly do your children like their praise?

12. Lion taming - blow marbles through a straw (a breathing technique).

13. Some threats of consequences are too big. Don't threaten to take away a huge trip as it's likely to be lost very quickly or it's too big for a child to see as an incentive.

14. Use a calming activity to help a child out of anger, deal with the consequences when they have calmed down. Try doing a jigsaw, reading a book or playing a ball game.

15. You have learnt to bargain your way out of situations; we do it all the time. Surely your children deserve to be taught that skill too?

16. Teach your children to feel good about themselves for doing things for other people, help them learn to get fulfilment and satisfaction just by helping someone else.

17. There is a risk of talking to a child about something too early and mentally taking them back there. This can cause the lion to appear again.

18. Agree as parents what causes of tantrums you are going to ignore. Agree what the level of behavior that can be ignored is and stick to it.

19. Timetables help structure school breaks and help avoid negative behavior. It can be as simple as on Monday we are going to the shops, Wednesday we are seeing Gran, Thursday we are going to the zoo; or as detailed as what to do in the morning.

20. Sometimes you need to walk away from a tantrum, sometimes you need to pick up your child and cuddle them, and sometimes you need to hold their hand.

21. Agree as a family the consequences for breaking the family rules, like early bedtime, lack of TV, missing out on a treat.

22. All behavior has a meaning, positive or negative. Understand what your child is saying to you, whether it's positive or negative behavior.

23. Sometimes it's useful to speak to someone outside the situation. Would it help if your child spoke to their grandparent on the phone? Would it help you?

24. What is the reward your child can earn by finding a good way out of anger?

25. It is acceptable to agree that your child can do something you are asking them to do later.

26. Lion taming - teaching your child relaxation phrases to use when angry helps to tame the lion.

27. By continuing your argument with your child, what do you want them to learn from it?

28. Negotiation is a life skill that we use daily; teach it to your children.

29. If someone stimulates a fear response in us, we are backed into a corner and use a fear solution. We don't like the feeling that we have been backed into a corner. Children are no different.

30. Make your house a competition to be the most successful, not the worst behaved. Inspire positive behavior!

31. Ask a child to do something once, give them thinking time before asking them again. Only put in a consequence after the third time of asking.

32. Repetitive physical actions help to calm us down, try bouncing a ball off the wall, a basketball up and down, throwing and catching a ball.

33. Unsafe ways of dealing with anger are acting out, dumping, withdrawal, bottling up or suppressing it.

34. Threats often make a child cross the line rather than stop themselves.

35. Lion taming - time-out helps us to self-regulate and in turn helps to tame the lion.

36. Think how it will make you child feel when they are thanked by a stranger for holding open a door.

37. Are there particular words that set your child off? What different words could you use?

38. Does your child need a hug or positive touch to help them deal with being overwhelmed?

39. Decide how important the cause of the tantrum is in the grand scheme of things, is it worth ruining the day for?

40. Family rules apply to adults too.

41. Make consequences realistic, taking away something or grounding a child for weeks and months is too long. If you are taking things away, just do it for short periods of time or let your children earn it back.

42. Distract your child by talking about something different.

43. Be like a swan when tackling negative behavior, even if you don't know what to do. Be calm and controlled on the outside even if you are swimming furiously underneath.

44. Sometimes children can only say sorry when they have calmed down.

45. Praise your child for using anger management techniques they have learnt. This turns a negative situation into a positive one.

46. Lion taming - giving children time to think before speaking or answering gives them a chance to take a deep breath and tame the lion.

47. Ask your child what they would like to do after a chore that makes them angry rather than tell them to do the chore and cause an argument.

48. Sorting or tidying a stack of things (like washing or pairing socks) is a great way of calming down.

49. Is there somewhere you can go as a family, where you can pull up and the children can run and let off steam?

50. Be specific about praise, if it's vague then it's meaningless.

51. Stay at the same level, if you start off being calm, remain calm, and if you start off being firm then be firm.

52. Have a family reward system, where the whole family benefits from you all being positive to each other. Putting pasta in a jar is a great way of letting your family see how they are succeeding and getting closer to the prize.

53. Lion taming - slow breathing helps reduce our pulse which tames the lion.

54. How do you recognize you are angry? How does your body feel? Have you ever taught your children how your body feels when you are angry?

55. Lion taming - teaching your child to meditate helps tame the lion.

56. Do you need time apart to both cool down?

57. Encourage your family to creatively problem solve things that normally cause people to become angry.

58. What behavior is just done to get a reaction out of you? That is behavior to ignore (remember you are the adult!).

59. Lion taming - verbalizing when to walk away.

60. Is there a different chore your child could do instead?

61. What relaxes you? Teach ways of relaxing to your children.

62. Lion taming - not holding grudges helps tame the lion.

63. Consider breaking a family prize into bits that each person is earning part of. It could be that you agree on a movie night and one child will earn the family popcorn, the other fizzy drinks.

64. Children only develop the skills to follow rules without external help, like rewards, sticker charts, parent's help, at the ages of 4 or 5.

65. Do you both need time out? Time out can be a consequence or a calm down technique.

66. Not everything you were taught as a child about anger management was right. How can you change things for your children?

67. Help build the resilience in your children to cope with the stresses and strains of life.

68. Saying sorry is important and should be meant. Adults need to say sorry too.

69. Lion taming - set up a reward system for keeping the anger lion away.

70. Lion taming - someone counting to ten and helping us breath slowly tames the lion.

71. Some children like being calmed by being rubbed on their head or spoken to softly. What relaxed your children when they were babies? It may still work when they are older too?

72. Try not to react when your children push your buttons.

73. We need to teach our children how to let some things go. It is too easy to hold a grudge. Think how awful you feel when you are holding a grudge and how it would make a child feel. Think how strong they will be being able to get over those feelings and learn to let things go.

74. Making someone laugh can break a tantrum.

75. Safe ways of dealing with anger are letting go, reflecting and expression.

76. We all get angry, it is a natural emotion. Have you spent time teaching your child to cope with it?

77. Distract your child from their tantrum by getting them to do something else until they calm down.

78. When you are angry, what do you do to calm yourself down and give yourself time to think? Do you clean, iron, wash dishes? What have you taught your children to do?

79. Use a tick chart to show your children what they need to do each day and empower them to track their success by ticking it off themselves.

80. When you lose control with a child and you don't know what to do you want to spank them. This is because you have lost control, not them.

81. Lion taming – teaching a child to ask for help helps tame the lion.

82. Do you need to play good cop/ bad cop with your partner to help your child find a way out of their anger?

83. When dealing with positive and negative behavior set the temperature, be the thermostat. Do not let them set the thermostat and let you be the temperature.

84. Lion taming - learning how our body reacts to anger helps know our reactions and helps tame the lion.

85. Get your children hooked on positive behavior, don't leave a void as they will find they can get hooked on negative behaviors.

86. Lion taming - going for a brisk walk or run helps to tame the lion.

87. How do you feel when people shout at you? How does a child feel?

88. Lion taming - teaching children what
    sensations are relaxing and safe to them
    (like snuggling under a blanket), allow
    children to learn to access them when they
    are angry and help tame the lion.

89. Lion taming - learning to blow up balloons
    or blow large bubbles helps us develop
    slow breathing to help tame the lion.

90. Children are not naughty; they do not have
    the skills to cope with the problem they
    are facing.

91. What behavior do you plan to ignore?

What behavior needs ignoring?

92. Have you taught your children how to recognise their lion, that they are getting angry and what to do when they feel their body reacting?

93. Children are not born knowing positive or negative behavior, it is a response to their experiences. We have a duty to form those experiences into positive ones.

94. Sometimes children can't put things right and all they can do is say sorry.

95. Ever tried whispering at someone who is angry?

96. Do you and your children play verbal tennis? Do the same words at the beginning of an argument result in the end being the same? If you find the outcome is predictable then change what you do and say at the beginning.

97. Lion taming - teaching a child to express anger through I statements helps to release the emotion and tame the lion (I feel tight in my tummy).

98. Boundaries are important, but sometimes we all need some flexibility.

99. Lion taming - repetitive physical actions help calm us, which tames the lion.

100.   Can you lead your child to a space to calm down when they are having a tantrum?

101.   Use a calm voice, tone, face and body shape when calming a tantrum.

Richard Curtis

Head on over to

101tipsforparents.com

for an exclusive thank you gift from

The Kid Calmer.

Richard Curtis

Tip index

ABOUT THE AUTHOR

Richard Curtis, the Kid Calmer, has devoted his life to understanding and working with children and families and is renowned for his experience with children with special needs and severe behavioral difficulties. He has influenced the lives of thousands of children around the globe and has developed an excellent reputation for understanding what different behaviors mean. Richard runs thekidcalmer.com, a website to help parents with their parenting dilemmas and share strategies that he has developed. He also is the founder of The Root Of It, a team of professionals who help schools, families and children.

Richard lives in Southampton, England and in his spare time keeps chickens, grows vegetables and runs a children's theatre group. He is a teacher, has earned a Master's Degree based on working with children with behavioral difficulties and also holds several specialist qualifications.

Printed in Great Britain
by Amazon